"Live

a way that it provokes questions for which the gospel is the answer."

Lesslie Newbigin

The Gospel in a Pluralist Society

"The most efficient means to spread an idea today is a corporate structure."

Jack Dorsey

Forbes magazine

THE REDEMPTIVE BUSINESS

A PLAYBOOK FOR LEADERS

TABLE OF CONTENTS

HOW TO USE THIS PLAYBOOK

We write for enterprising leaders in small- to medium-sized, privately-held companies who see business as an endeavor with moral significance and cultural power.

You know your work in business *means* something, and you want your organization to be a force for good. That's a tall order in a highly competitive arena full of ethically questionable norms, scarce resources, competitive pressures, and shifting cultural expectations.

Still, you are drawn to the entrepreneurial journey, in part because it holds so much promise: though you have to work within this system with all its strengths and flaws, you hope to build something new, beautiful, and lasting.

At Praxis we have worked closely with hundreds of entrepreneurs like this: founders, teams, and funders of growing businesses, where the leaders know their investors and have the prerogative to set vision, make strategic and operational decisions, build teams, and allocate capital with a high degree of autonomy. These leaders—and those who aspire to follow in their footsteps—are the primary audience for this book.

We are a community dedicated to putting our Christian faith into practice through redemptive entrepreneurship—in our leadership behavior and in the products, services, and organizations we build. That faith empowers redemptive entrepreneurs to pursue the good of others from within the market system, precisely because of their ultimate allegiance outside it.

This should be good news for everyone. Indeed, we believe that enterprising leaders who are spiritually serious, culturally astute, and embedded in accountable communities are uniquely suited for entrepreneurial work that makes the world a more just and humanizing place for all.

So, though this book is not exclusively *for* Christians, it is written *to* Christians, as it is rooted in Christian conceptions of human identity, purpose, and the common good.

The playbook is structured in two main parts: a First Principles essay, followed by six sections covering areas of business that we believe are most vital to redemptive impact: Products, Brand, Culture, Business Model, Partnerships, and Ambition. In each Commitment area we suggest several "redemptive opportunities"—actionable principles that you can adapt and apply in your venture.

Some of these may feel natural or even second-nature; others may seem purely aspirational. We hope to introduce tension where you are complacent, clarity where you are confused, and hope where you are jaded.

After reading the playbook alone or with a team, we suggest that you work through the six areas one at a time. Use the text first for assessment and discussion—identifying areas of strength, weakness, and possibility. Then choose one or two where you sense the greatest energy, and use them as a starting point for adaptation, prototyping, and designing your own creative ways to approach the redemptive edge of your venture's mission.

FIRST PRINCIPLES

Any conversation about business in the 21st century takes place within the history of capitalism, a system that has been fantastically successful globally on its own terms, has materially improved the lives of billions, and has also entrenched various kinds of exploitation in ways great and small, old and new.

Our view is that capitalism, the markets that fund it, and the business practices based upon it, are both good and corruptible. We know of no other economic system in our imperfect world that can produce such prosperity, liberty, and satisfaction by allowing us to use our gifts, pursue our interests, collaborate through self-organizing communities, and generate value for our fellow humans.

At the same time, precisely because of its social and economic potency, and its invitation to power and wealth, business has also proven to be an enabler of widespread harm, exclusion, and exploitative extraction of value. Though markets can offer us virtuous incentives to meet the needs of certain groups, they can also generate perverse incentives to exploit and exclude others.

And while each generation eradicates some of the worst business practices of earlier eras, it manages to introduce new ones in their wake. We still live in an age of sweatshops, predatory sales practices, financial fraud, environmental degradation, and racial inequity. Some of today's most profitable and highly capitalized businesses are predicated on leveraging their customers' attention and privacy, or their workers' vulnerability, with astonishing levels of sophistication and misdirection. Workplaces remain the site of millions of small daily indignities, visited on fellow human beings in every area of business from contract negotiations to team dynamics.

This fundamental tension at the heart of capitalism—its proven power for social good entwined with its legacy of harm—has been present since Adam Smith articulated its principles and limitations in the 18th century. In the 1970s, economist Milton Friedman famously proposed that the "social responsibility of a business is to increase its profits," so as to maximize shareholder value. In this view, society is best served through a single, clear accountability to investors, who in enlightened self-interest work through rational markets to reward organizations that benefit the world over the long run.

Business should work like that, but it so often doesn't. Indeed, ever since Friedman's view was codified, reformers have sprung up to challenge and moderate it, offering such alternatives as "creative capitalism," "shared value capitalism," "conscious capitalism," "compassionate capitalism," "inclusive capitalism," "completing capitalism," and so on. These all reflect two widespread convictions about the purpose of business.

First, it seems we want to live in a society in which organizations carry obligations not only to their present shareholders, but also to current and future stakeholders—employees, customers, shareholders, partners, and communities. Second, these obligations cannot be adequately valued or incentivized through financial metrics alone, and therefore a more comprehensive and balanced accounting of the impact of a business (often referred to as a multiple bottom line) is needed.

Companies such as Whole Foods, Chobani, and Patagonia were prophets of this "stakeholder capitalism" view from their inception, and scaled their philosophy into the world as they succeeded on the market's terms. Likewise, ventures in the social entrepreneurship sector, or those in the B Corp movement, are defined by their rigorous pursuit of social, cultural, and environmental impact metrics alongside financial ones. The stakeholder view is moving toward the mainstream, and is now espoused—at least publicly—by many of today's most prominent institutional investors and corporate leaders.

While there is still plenty of room for debate on the best regulatory, governance, or equity arrangements, redemptive business leaders are stakeholder capitalists in heart and practice. We view God—not our investors, and certainly not ourselves—as the ultimate source of accountability. We are called to love our neighbors, create lasting cultural products, and steward the resources of creation, whatever kind of business we are in. So whether running a fashion brand, offering cleaning services to homeowners, developing enterprise software, leading a healthcare startup, manufacturing appliances, or launching a restaurant—we are to care for every stakeholder of the business as part of our mission.

That said, we are confronted every day with two central myths of business: the *supremacy of money* and the *inevitability of progress*. The first of these, simply, is that the bottom line is the bottom line. Nearly every decision will test and reveal the leaders' ultimate view of money—namely, in this business, is money a means or an end? Regardless of what we say about our people, mission, and values, do we feel so beholden to "the money" that financial considerations exert downward pressure on every element of the enterprise? Are financial returns in the short or medium term the one non-negotiable factor that must always be maximized, or are they one vital factor to be optimized among several? Does doing the right thing simply mean to forgo some profit today with the expectation of greater profit later, or are we free to make certain decisions according to other convictions, knowing that "the right thing" could actually limit profits over time?

Many founders never allow themselves to ask these questions, instead defaulting to short-term, finance-first views based on the prominent examples of publicly-traded or venture-backed companies. They make plans and raise funds with a preset, constrained view of money, time, and growth for their enterprise. Certainly an unprofitable business cannot be redemptive (as it will cease to exist). Yet at the other extreme, a business designed to be maximally profitable in the near term is likely to fall short of its greatest potential impact on employees, customers, and partners.

As with the supremacy of money, redemptive entrepreneurs must confront another myth that is embedded just as deeply in our present-day system of enterprise: the *inevitability of progress*.

This myth says that development is always, on the whole, improvement. If we are able to accomplish general technological and productivity advances, we are led to believe, the good life is just over the horizon. But we can now see how incomplete this view is. To be sure, the jobs created by capitalism have reduced global poverty and turned a fortunate billion human beings or so into the wealthiest generation in the history of the world—yet many of these blessings have been secured at the exclusion or expense of vulnerable groups. What's more, we are not just material beings.

Though we carry supercomputers in our pockets, just 12% of Americans enjoy their jobs; life expectancy, social capital, and attention spans are shrinking; and suicide, addiction, and depression among our youth have reached levels never before seen.

As we build out mass automation, machine learning, genetic modification, and other historic breakthroughs, it is by no means clear that these developments will in fact produce more human flourishing. Indeed, to believe so requires something approaching blind faith. Indeed, even a noble social mission—say, "to give people the power to build community and bring the world closer together," the corporate mission statement of Facebook—can coexist with (and legitimize) notoriously extractive practices with customers and partners. (Almost always, such moves are made in the service of money, prioritizing profits or user growth over the actual flourishing of those very users. This is an example of how the supremacy of money and the inevitability of progress reinforce one another.)

Redemptive business leaders celebrate and leverage certain trends, while actively resisting others that are out of line with their convictions about human flourishing. They are not satisfied only to profit on the system's terms; their greater ambition is to act as prophets of a better way. In fact, some of the most redemptive leaders not only create new products, services, and business models that take advantage of the "rules of the game," they also have the sacrificial and prophetic imagination to challenge those rules for the benefit of others.

Let's explore in more depth what it means to be redemptive, and how this powerful idea lies behind our entrepreneurial calling.

We use a tool called The Redemptive Frame to define and explore redemptive possibilities in organizational or vocational settings. It combines the Three Ways to Work with the Three Dimensions of Work.

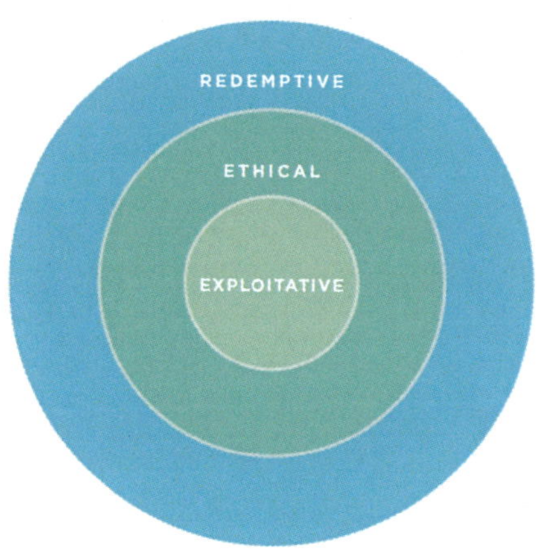

THE REDEMPTIVE FRAME: THREE WAYS TO WORK

People, organizations, or communities approach the world in one of three ways.

The Exploitative way is to *take all you can get*—to gain any advantage, to prevail, to possess. Exploitative actors most often approach the business with a zero-sum, "I win, you lose" scarcity mentality. The motivating force behind the Exploitative way is to win and control.

We are surrounded by the Exploitative way; we all fall naturally into it; and we are always trying to escape its effects on us.

The Ethical way is to *do things right*—to do no harm, keep the rules, solve problems, add value. Ethical actors pursue "win-win" whenever they can. The motivating force behind the Ethical way is to be good.

We expect the Ethical of ourselves and of those around us, yet we sometimes fall short; and we're grateful when we encounter it.

The Redemptive way is *creative restoration through sacrifice*—to bless others, renew culture, and give of ourselves. Redemptive actors pursue an "I sacrifice, we win" approach with the agency and resources available to them. The motivating force behind the Redemptive way is to love and serve.

We rarely expect to encounter the Redemptive; though whenever we do, we're changed.

But what does it really mean to be Redemptive? And why does it never fail to change us?

DEFINING REDEMPTIVE

The Christian account is that God created humanity in his image—so even though we are more frail and proud than we are willing to admit, we are more loved and worthy than we can imagine.

Our shared cultural work—to bear God's image in the world by creating and cultivating with the resources he gave us—is distorted by our selfishness, and cannot be put fully right through human efforts alone.

Yet putting the world right—bringing about personal, spiritual, social, cultural, and environmental healing and restoration—is part of God's loving and glorious purpose in the world he created. As people loved through grace, we are called to love God and neighbor by joining him in that work.

Redemption is an economic term that means to buy back something (or someone) to restore it to its rightful place. It is also used to describe Jesus' act of sacrificing his life so that we can be ultimately restored to a right relationship with God and his creation. Wherever there is loss, brokenness, unfairness, waste, or harm—and someone willingly enters into the situation by bearing a cost or taking a risk to help the person, resource, or system to be restored—that's redemptive action. And redemptive action at any scale usually requires creation or innovation, such as a new product, expression, model, or norm.

We respond to the redemptive, in stories and especially in real life, because we know that the world is broken; because we long to participate in its healing, even in the smallest ways; and because we sense that sacrificial love is the world's most powerful force.

So this core pattern—creative restoration through sacrifice—not only describes Jesus' ultimate redemptive work to save the world but also our daily redemptive work to serve the world. It gives shape to our mission as those who have been written into the greater story of his purposes through no merit of our own.

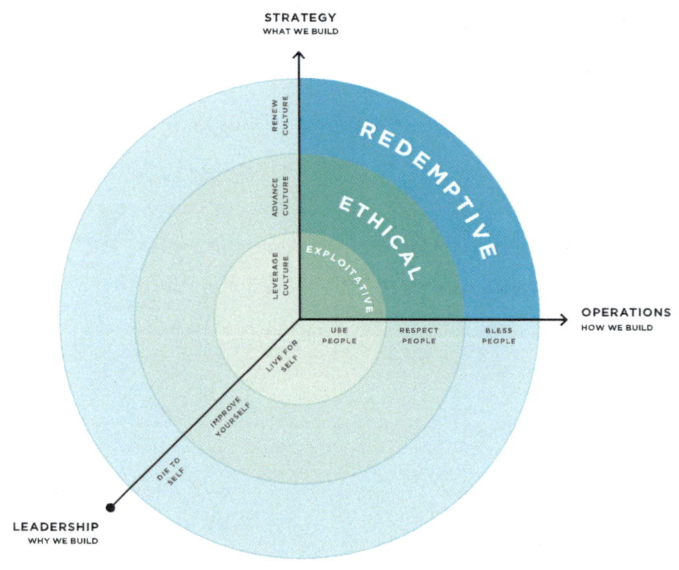

THE REDEMPTIVE FRAME: THREE DIMENSIONS OF WORK

Strategy centers on *what we build.* It's everything a business does to express mission, serve customers, and create value—in the form of products, services, programs, brands, and even digital and physical experiences. We define Strategy by its *cultural impact.*

Redemptive Strategy doesn't exploit or leverage cultural trends for gain, or even merely advance culture in the direction of progress. Instead, it is products, services, programs, brands, and experiences that renew culture to be more humanizing, truthful, beautiful, lasting, and God-glorifying.

Operations centers on *how we build*. It's everything a business does to develop, support, and deliver the Strategy in the form of culture, systems, capital and other assets, business models, innovation, and partnerships. We define Operations by its *people impact.*

Redemptive Operations refuses to use people merely as resources to achieve organizational goals; and it seeks to go further than merely respecting team members and partners. Instead, it is culture, business models, capital stewardship, and partnerships that bless people through grace, generosity, justice, patience, and mutuality.

Leadership centers on *why we build.* It's the motives, ambition, worldview, character, and imagination of the leadership team—which set the course and define the horizons of possibility for the venture's Strategy and Operations. We define Leadership by its *success script.*

Redemptive Leadership is marked not by an ambition to *live for ourselves*, or even just to *improve ourselves*. Instead, it is patiently rewiring our motives, worldview, imagination, and practices around dying to self—becoming more surrendered, accountable, rested, and generous.

DEFINING REDEMPTIVE ENTREPRENEURSHIP

Redemptive entrepreneurship

is building

creative restoration through sacrifice

into the world

through our vocations & organizations.

A REDEMPTIVE IMAGINATION FOR BUSINESS

Despite the disheartening areas of brokenness, we come down firmly on the side of business as a worthy vocation and a vehicle for meaningful service, impact, and deep joy. So much innovation genuinely contributes to human flourishing, and there are ways to benefit from money's liquidity, exchange, and accounting value without granting it a supreme place. We believe that redemptive entrepreneurship is a profoundly "disruptive innovation"—a way to bring the upside-down reality of the kingdom of God to the world. Organizations led in this way can serve people at scale through the unique power of modern markets, while working against the exploitation of all stakeholders—teams, investors, partners, customers, and even competitors.

If this vision of creative restoration through sacrifice is consistently lived out, we will see transformation in every industry. Redemptive leaders will invite their teams, boards, investors, and community to keep them accountable to remain aligned with missional purposes. Our organizations will become pacesetters for rebuilding the squandered reserves of trust that are so essential to productive markets—and provide workplaces where people are challenged, developed, and truly known. The entrepreneurial ecosystem will become radically more equitable in how it enables access to capital, talent, and opportunity. We will all partake of the cultural benefits of having more of the next generation's most able minds focused on solutions to consequential problems. We will see in our neighbors' lives the downstream effects of products, services, and brands that redefine the good life away from individual consumption and toward contentment and community.

By fixing their imagination on what is lasting—even eternal—entrepreneurs can be among the greatest contributors to the common good here and now.

COMMITMENTS OF THE REDEMPTIVE BUSINESS

REDEMPTIVE STRATEGY

We develop products, services, and experiences that genuinely benefit our customers, their communities, and the world; and we thoughtfully minimize downside consequences. We avoid manipulative design or sales practices that profit the company but erode broader societal trust.

We craft a brand through imagination and truth, advancing narratives of virtue and hope across our venture's sphere of influence. We resist the urge to play to our customers' desires, insecurity, or ego through marketing based on fear or status.

REDEMPTIVE OPERATIONS

We advance a team culture that helps people experience their work as neither ultimate nor transactional, but as purposeful and relational. We develop each person for and beyond their contribution to our mission instead of treating them merely as resources to advance the organization's interests.

Our business model optimizes for measurable value that is shared with customers and partners, not captured solely for the business and its owners. It takes into account social and environmental benefits and costs as well as the responsible management of financial capital and profit that is essential to a lasting business.

We grow through partnerships of mutuality and integrity, avoiding a zero-sum view that only considers our own organizational priorities. We treat our investors, suppliers, distributors, and all partners as we would like to be treated, considering the needs, pressures, and health of their businesses and communities.

REDEMPTIVE LEADERSHIP

We surrender our personal ambition to God and seek first the good of others, not ourselves. Instead of privately yielding our desires to an accumulation of wealth, power, and prestige, we cultivate gratitude, joy, and humility in the way we lead and serve.

PRODUCTS

WE DEVELOP PRODUCTS, SERVICES, AND EXPERIENCES THAT GENUINELY BENEFIT OUR CUSTOMERS

SUMMARY

We develop products, services, and experiences that genuinely benefit our customers, their communities, and the world; and we thoughtfully minimize downside consequences. We avoid manipulative design or sales practices that profit the company but erode broader societal trust.

OUR REALITY

Our society's appetite for innovation and optimization in technology and product development means that we expect every cycle to deliver us better, faster, and cheaper—in every category. Disciplines as diverse as psychology, machine learning, behavioral economics, and biomechanics have been incorporated into product design. The result has been a generation of products, services, and experiences that are more sophisticated—and more influential on our daily routines, perspectives, expectations, and social norms—than any before imaginable.

Indeed, almost nothing in our interactions with products and services is left to chance. We have learned to productize everything, from consumer devices to business services to smartphone apps to financial instruments to physical experiences. Everything is carefully designed and bundled; the question is, to what end?

The answer is increasingly disquieting. We live in the shadow of the subprime mortgages of the 2008 financial crisis, and of the arresting technologies deployed by social media giants and their descendants in the years since. These and other examples are opening our eyes to the realization that the evolving disciplines of design, technology, and financial engineering are being used to ensnare us as much as to liberate us. For example, our personal data is regularly used against us to weaken our defenses of self-control and discernment.

How did we get here? Unfortunately, more often than not, entrepreneurs and their investors have chosen user and revenue growth at nearly all costs—pursuing shorter-term profits over what is healthiest for our customers, employees, and communities. In part this is because our contemporary economy has been engineered around the dangerous idea that we and our neighbors are defined by our consumption. The default ethos of the startup world is to "make something people want," which suggests that human desire is nearly always worth satisfying, even maximizing. In this economy, some of the "best" products are those that marshal design, brand, and business model innovation to appeal to our most self-centered, lonely, addictive tendencies.

Instead, we long to make *what people want to want*—products and services that help us see ourselves and relate to our neighbors as whole persons, rather than merely as monetizable units of desire, consumption, and metadata production.

REDEMPTIVE OPPORTUNITIES

1. We pursue impact/market fit, not merely product/market fit, in each category we serve. Seeking to embody our mission through our offerings, we focus on the intended impact on the individual, community, and society as our explicit design objective. We then develop products, services, experiences, and business models that can reliably and profitably deliver that impact.

2. We design our products, services, and even physical spaces with our customers as partners and co-designers of our work, not only as its subjects or buyers. We regularly invite diverse perspectives from beyond our most profitable customer segments to shape our imagination for design and impact.

3. We bring products, services, and experiences to market with the intention and commitment that they will routinely deliver customer value that exceeds the promise. We design and build physical and digital products for segment-leading quality and durability.

4. We surround our products with sales, marketing, and delivery processes that explicitly build trust as a key value proposition to customers. When we break trust, we work sacrificially to restore it. This commitment not only benefits us; it also helps to replenish the depleted reservoirs of trust necessary for our markets and societies to thrive.

5. We bring products to market only after a thorough, prayerful, and imaginative contemplation of their potential negative impacts on customers, communities, and the environment. We actively refine offerings to minimize their downsides, and generously serve those most likely to experience them.

6. We develop a thesis statement addressing our mission, desired impact, and theory of change. This establishes alignment and accountability to our purpose and impact, and provides opportunity to bear witness to our underlying redemptive commitments.

THE GOOD NEWS

As a people committed to a countercultural account of what it is to be human—of our origin, identity, purpose, and destiny as eternal persons—we have the opportunity to deliver more fully and truly on the promise of the innovation process often known as human-centered design. We can develop products and services based on careful attention to the needs and capabilities of persons made in God's image, with profitability a test of value and viability rather than the end that justifies the means.

Our design faculties can be re-animated through the challenges of discovering new ways to delight, to ennoble, to connect, to empower. As our teams grow in this mindset and approach, we will be able to see the flourishing of our customers as fundamental to our mission, not just as a means to profitability or survival.

We can enjoy a healthy relationship with our products and services, holding them with the proper weight and importance. On one hand, we won't treat our offerings with the messianic obsession of some celebrated entrepreneurs who, even in pursuit of a compelling mission, elevate the product or service to an idolatrous level of meaning-making. On the other hand, we will be less prone to lapse into treating our products merely as pragmatic means to the ends of perpetuating our organization and its economic engine. Instead, we can create and cultivate our company's offerings as artifacts and expressions that are worth our care, excellence, and endeavor.

BRAND

WE CRAFT A BRAND OF VIRTUE AND HOPE THROUGH IMAGINATION AND TRUTH

SUMMARY

We craft a brand through imagination and truth, advancing narratives of virtue and hope across our venture's sphere of influence. We resist the urge to play to our customers' desires, insecurity, or ego through marketing based on fear or status.

OUR REALITY

At the heart of every business are brand stories—origin narratives, customer pain points, fresh insights into a systemic issue, inspired pivots, new opportunities for impact. Over time, these stories evolve into an organizational narrative that propels vision, products, teams, and resources into reality.

These stories are important and good, for it is deeply satisfying to tap into meaningful human experience through our brand. Yet human beings don't just tell stories, we also make *myths*—grand narratives that promise to unlock the truth about the world. And in today's business environment, it often feels like it is not enough to have a good story—you need to craft a myth of epic proportions in order to stand out from the crowd and win the loyalty of a generation of consumers who are hungry for meaning and identity.

And so we are tempted to greatly exaggerate the origin, the current reality, and the ultimate scope of our work. We may retell our venture story in ways that amplify our obstacles, minimize our privilege, and position us as heroes when the reality may be less flattering and more mundane. Our marketing can feed our customers' self-concept in similar ways.

We may find ourselves competing with companies that oversell both the actual capabilities and the social meaning of their work, and we are tempted to raise our stakes accordingly. Instead of casting an inspiring vision that we can actually deliver upon, we trumpet our work's ability to deliver "the good life" for our customers, orienting ownership and experiences to the deepest human longings and implying a level of fulfillment that is beyond any product, service, or firm's ability to deliver.

These myths regularly collapse in spectacular and tragic fashion—witness the firms that promised community but instead fed polarization, that proclaimed a new "we" but actually enriched a single "me," that stood for happiness but whose leaders were plagued by addiction and self-destructiveness. And new brands with new myths are always taking their place. It is incredibly hard to believe that we could succeed by simply telling the truth, about ourselves, our customers, and our products, and that our imagination could be realistic and achievable rather than fantastical and idolatrous.

Instead, we long for the chance to tell good, true, and beautiful stories that will not ultimately betray us or those who trusted in them. We long to convey the possibility of real good here on earth, even as we still acknowledge that every human myth grasps for a greater good that is only found in God.

REDEMPTIVE OPPORTUNITIES

1. We thoughtfully maximize our opportunity to rewrite a cultural narrative, particularly in categories where exploitative messages or products have been normalized and there is a need to expose harm, recapture truth, or shift expectations.

2. We root out brand hyperbole, refusing to establish false needs or implicit promises that our products or services claim to address or fulfill. Our brand promise—

what we suggest our venture and offerings can reliably deliver to customers and partners over time—is a true reflection of what we are designing and operating the business to deliver on its best day.

3. We base our brand narrative on an eternal understanding of identity and worth that is not conferred through consumption, group affiliation, or self-expression, but through inherent human dignity, relationships, and virtue. We address our current and potential customers as whole people bearing great responsibilities, struggles, and capacities, who long for deep meaning and close community that businesses cannot fully provide.

4. We ensure that our brand story runs on contentment over materialism; trust over suspicion; interdependence over individualism; hope over wishful thinking; wisdom over fear; and freedom over compulsion.

5. We carefully consider whose voices, faces, stories, and experiences will represent our brand. Rather than relying on comfortable stereotypes or making inauthentic

displays of diversity, we foreground people who represent our brand's community at its best and fullest.

6. We are truthful and gracious with all constituencies in our communications—customers, board, investors, partners, team, the public, and even competitors. We openly acknowledge failure, naming what we have learned without spreading blame; and we generously celebrate others rather than elevating ourselves at their expense.

THE GOOD NEWS

This is the area of the business in which we have the greatest opportunity to demonstrate that one of our ultimate "products" is trust. In that light, our branding and marketing teams will discover that finding creative ways to tell the truth requires just as much skill and craft, and is far more satisfying, than finding creative ways to shade the truth. Indeed, our first step in redemptive branding is often to attend to the simple satisfactions delivered by our product or service. To the extent that we can creatively help people revel in what our offering actually does, we can resist the temptation to hook our brand up to inflated promises of what it can never really do.

As trust and value grows in the enterprise alongside financial sustainability, our company's brand will become an authentic platform for contribution to a positive narrative about how the world ought to be. Advertising budgets, PR, and other impressions of our work will become opportunities to share redemptive stories and vision, and encourage customers to share in the future that the company seeks to build.

If "whoever tells the best story wins," then as people committed to what we believe is a truer and better story than any other, we can be confident in our brand narrative—even in the places where it is modest. To the extent it advances a mission aligned with the heart of God, and honors humanity as reflective of his image, it will bear the imprint of the true Good News—and we can know we are serving our neighbor by telling our story to the world.

CULTURE

WE ADVANCE A TEAM CULTURE THAT MAKES WORK PURPOSEFUL AND RELATIONAL

SUMMARY

We advance a team culture that helps people experience their work as neither ultimate nor transactional, but as purposeful and relational. We develop each person for and beyond their contribution to our mission instead of treating them merely as resources to advance the organization's interests.

OUR REALITY

Every organization intends to attract great people, build a healthy culture, and develop great leaders—yet most organizations fall well short in actual practice.

Particularly through the influence of the technology and knowledge sectors, we are all being pushed into *workism*, to borrow the coinage of Derek Thompson—in which our work carries too much weight in forming our sense of value and purpose. From the always-hustling culture of Silicon Valley to the Chinese "996" norm of working from 9 to 9, 6 days a week, there is an expectation that if you really want to rise, more work is always better. And if work defines our identity, how can we refuse? Under the promise of "always-on" access and maximal productivity, we rarely have a moment where our inbox or most pressing work issue is absent from our minds. And our workism can affect others even more than ourselves: as those of us with the most margin and agency willingly exploit ourselves, we create norms that flow downstream to those with far fewer choices.

Organizational culture suffers when our work means too much, and also when it means too little. A companion error to workism is *instrumentalism*—the view that work is merely a means to money and freedom. Here too, organizations and individuals can conspire in what seems little more than an exchange of labor for money. Leaders use people as "human resources" to be allocated rather than as whole persons to be developed and blessed, perhaps especially in environments where the opportunities for impact or financial returns are significant. We may "invest" in our people's usefulness to our venture, but this language can feel hollow if we demonstrate little regard for their lives outside or beyond their tenure at the organization.

Almost all human communities tend toward conformity and avoid confronting the most difficult truths, and our workplaces easily become places where certain truths are never spoken and many voices are never heard. As we pare down our ranks to those who are willing and able to tolerate an organizational monoculture, our firms gradually lose the honest edge at which real excellence is found. We may recruit and retain for a conventional "good fit" in ways that exclude the abundant diversity of human experience and limit our organization's capacity for generative growth.

Instead, we long for our organizational culture to reflect grace and truth; and for members of our team to bring their whole selves to work and be energized by their work for their whole lives. We aim to create workplace cultures that cultivate and celebrate redemptive action, blessing people by giving more than we ask in return.

REDEMPTIVE OPPORTUNITIES

1. We steward people for and beyond the work of the organization, beginning with uncommonly thoughtful hiring processes, and making every effort to design assignments and development paths that balance each individual's goals with business needs. Where people are not succeeding, we act quickly, first adjusting for better alignment internally, and if necessary, guiding and supporting them generously in leaving the organization.

2. We cultivate a "high excellence, high grace" ethos in our communications, decisions, and actions. We speak the truth in love through redemptive feedback—honest, developmental, and honoring.

3. We guard our culture by celebrating stories of redemptive and mission-aligned action, from the CFO to the intern; and by privately admonishing exploitative behavior, up to and including the termination of persistently damaging actors, no matter their seniority or influence.

4. We honor each team member through our HR practices, with a bias for generosity in compensation, equity, benefits, agreements, and resources that extend trust and enable people to commit wholeheartedly to their work in light of all aspects of their vocations.

5. We invest intentionally and search beyond default talent sources to build a robust diversity of experience, gender, ethnic heritage, skill set, and viewpoints at every level of the organization—seeking not only to improve our organizational performance, but also to embody the fullest possible picture of God's glory in humanity.

6. We embody an ethos of principled public pluralism, where the expression of ultimate beliefs based on any (or no) faith is welcomed as essential to valuing the whole person; where spiritual resources such as corporate chaplaincy are offered non-coercively; and where the faith of the leaders is neither hidden nor culturally favored, and can be experienced by anyone as good news.

7. We practice healthy and sustainable work rhythms, encouraging intentional patterns of daily, weekly, and seasonal disconnection and rest. We encourage paid and flexible leave for parents and caregivers to devote themselves to those dependent on them.

THE GOOD NEWS

We can experience the profound satisfaction of loving and blessing people through all aspects of our organization. This work is not primarily a means to the end of organizational success—it is an end in itself, equally valuable in the sight of God as anything else we might accomplish through our products, services, or corporate social responsibility. Though we will stumble at times, we can be confident that our commitment to people for their own sake will be a compelling witness to our redemptive vision among the company's employees, investors, and partners.

We can accomplish so much good by counteracting instrumentalism and workism in our culture. Our team members will be able to exert their creative best in service to the mission, all while working within sustainable margins over the long term, and accepting whatever outcomes may follow. And we as leaders will also sense our own greater freedom through this promise.

Our resolve to build teams that reflect true unity-in-diversity will set us on a path of inevitable discomfort, setbacks, and missed opportunities. Yet our vision for diversity will stretch beyond the conventional organizational benefits (in the form of greater innovation, resilience, and access to talent). Indeed, we can proceed in the hope that together we are becoming a humble expression of the beloved community and a demonstration of the reconciling power of the gospel.

BUSINESS MODEL

OUR BUSINESS MODEL OPTIMIZES FOR SHARED VALUE

SUMMARY

Our business model optimizes for measurable value that is shared with customers and partners, not captured solely for the business and its owners. It takes into account social and environmental benefits and costs as well as the responsible management of financial capital and profit that is essential to a lasting business.

OUR REALITY

We can never afford to be disconnected from the role of money in our business; so we pay constant attention to cash flow, burn rate, margin, and other financially derived performance metrics. During seasons of fundraising we can be consumed with yielding the least control to get the most capital; and in seasons of strategic and operational planning there is some financial implication to every scenario and decision. These dynamics have always been present for enterprise builders.

Yet today, the finance sector has affected every growing business, regardless of how it is capitalized, by normalizing the expectations of return maximization—faster growth, higher returns, and earlier exits. While this has been productive at a macroeconomic level and enabled a rarefied class of startup "winners," it has also borne troubling fruit for many leaders and ventures, creating finance-driven practices that lead to team burnout, alienated customers, socially damaging business practices, and squandered value.

In this heightened race toward profitability or growth, we can easily lose sight of the vital balance between profit and the purposes it exists to enable. When we design and execute on a business model—value propositions, unit economics, revenue streams, pricing structures, practices for customer acquisition and retention, and economies of scale—our choices will lead to much more than just financial outcomes.

For example, many "attractive" business models rely on below-living-wage labor under conditions tantamount to slavery (much of fashion), non-renewable extraction from the environment (much of food and energy), or even the long-term elimination of the business's own workforce (much of the "gig economy"). These models spot purely financial opportunity within the lines of established systems of power (and often exploitation). Even when businesses constructed on these models become aware of abuses located outside their direct operations, they often are so dependent on those external systems that they cannot effectively confront or exit from them.

Furthermore, in some sectors, aggressive goal-setting—especially when tied to compensation and promotion—can have a perverse effect. This practice leads people to behave as though all that matters (above some minimal legal baseline) is the transaction and the bottom-line results. While incentive-driven models are becoming more common, these often lead to trickle-down damage on corporate culture, customer care, and even the mental and relational health of the team members affected. In the worst cases, such purely financial incentives become institutionalized in such a way that even the business's own leaders lose control of the behaviors of their workers. The "winners" of such a system add so much profit that they are untouchable because "they make too much money for the firm."

Instead, we long for deliverance from the distortions of treating money as supreme. We steward it as the essential fuel that allows our business to deliver sustained value—in financial and non-financial terms—for all stakeholders.

REDEMPTIVE OPPORTUNITIES

1. We operate with transparency in valuing and pricing our products and services, entrusting our customers with uncommon visibility into how we seek to make a fair profit.

2. We take great care with the integrity of our supply chain. We design and operate it not solely for financial optimization, or even merely to appeal to customer expectations, but to actively curtail the exploitation of persons and natural resources.

3. We set sustainable growth and pace targets that honor our stakeholder commitments—not only to our investors but also to our customers, our team, and the communities in which we operate. We plan for intentional seasons of more modest growth to build capacities in R&D, team, and infrastructure that will allow us to grow over the long run.

4. As a leadership team we actively model financial decision-making that prioritizes people. We invest in

our team's fluency with our financial model, believing that a more widespread understanding of our profit drivers will lead to more prudent decisions that conserve capital and preserve our mission over the long term.

5. Though our management system of goals and metrics drives action and accountability at the team and individual level, we carefully limit the use of direct performance-based incentives for individuals, recognizing the often perverse effects on workers, teams, customers, and even families.

6. We invite team participation and visibility into the ways we use our profits for long-term reinvestment in the business and generous mission-aligned corporate philanthropy.

THE GOOD NEWS

As leaders pursuing both faithfulness and impact, we can develop a healthier relationship to the goals and dynamics of growth. We can begin by challenging the common assumption that all businesses should seek to scale as much as possible. We know that many healthy small businesses grow consistently, serve their customers and communities well, and never achieve significant scale. And we must remember that in God's upside-down economy, bigger does not necessarily mean more blessing, importance, or honor.

Freed from the trap of letting others determine our financial model or growth curve, we can set our own course in light of our capabilities, ambition, priorities, and constraints. We will wisely consider what scale, reach, replication, and impact means—and doesn't mean—for our organization. From there, we can contemplate one of the most important and overlooked questions about profit: what is the right amount?

Indeed, we will be reoriented to a more purposeful understanding of the relationship between why we exist and how we exist. Instead of serving and satisfying customers in order to win and grow, we are free to grow so that we may serve and satisfy more customers, partners, and team members. Instead of inheriting business models that enshrine existing inequity, we can seek to design new ones that create entrenched good. We can hope to experience God-given satisfaction in mastering the art and science behind our financial engine, never forgetting that the business model is made for people, not people for the business model.

PARTNERSHIPS

WE GROW THROUGH PARTNERSHIPS OF MUTUALITY AND INTEGRITY

SUMMARY

We grow through partnerships of mutuality and integrity, avoiding a zero-sum view that only considers our own organizational priorities. We treat our investors, suppliers, distributors, and all partners as we would like to be treated, considering the needs, pressures, and health of their businesses and communities.

OUR REALITY

No business is an island. Modern economies are so highly interdependent that building a business is less about marshaling our "own" resources and more about entering into partnerships of many kinds—for capital, for channel and brand extension, across the supply chain, as well as for talent and other services.

Yet we must acknowledge the shadow side of this evolution. Just as financially maximized business models often reduce our people to abstract units of production, expertly arranged and cost-minimized to deliver on performance targets, we often treat external partners even more transactionally—as inputs to our success rather than value creators and potentially redemptive actors in their own right.

When we view service providers as interchangeable and disposable, we miss opportunities to strengthen each other's business. It is common to use requests for proposals (RFPs) and other bidding techniques to exert maximal pressure on vendors' prices and terms, turning a blind eye to the exploitation we may be driving them to adopt in order to win our business. With brand, channel, and supply chain partners, we may be more conscious of the opportunity for mutual benefit; nevertheless, we are taught to fight to get the better end of every deal and leave a disproportionate share of risk with our "partner."

If we desire outside capital and are able to source it, our partnerships with investors can be the most fraught of all. A generation ago, the main source of working capital for many enterprises was community banks. These investments were built on mutual, often lifelong, relationships anchored in ties to particular places. While this system was not perfect and often perpetuated patterns of exclusion, the decline of community banking has allowed an even more transactional system to arise, modeled on the venture capital funding model that has reshaped the tech world. Entrepreneurs in sectors far from tech's unique scaling economics have learned to sell an oversized story to attract investor attention, and investors expect to be oversold. As a result, too many investor/CEO relationships that begin with exaggeration (if not deception) never evolve beyond asymmetry and alienation. CEOs can treat potential investors as checkbooks instead of whole persons, either granting them false and unhealthy influence over our vision, priorities, and plans—or keeping them at a distance that limits relationship and accountability.

So we end up not as real partners with our vendors, collaborators, and investors, but as wary practitioners of "coopetition," constantly circling for advantage. We make unreasonable demands, pit potential partners against one another, and issue threats in order to "win" all negotiations; game the timing of payments as arbitrage; and when things go wrong, activate the most punitive terms possible.

Instead, we long to model and experience true partnership in every dimension of our business: high levels of trust and mutuality that lead to extraordinary performance in the good times and lifesaving resilience for each party in times of scarcity.

REDEMPTIVE OPPORTUNITIES

1. With a bias toward abundance and trust, we negotiate in good faith consideration of our partners' goals, constraints, and expectations—and are transparent about our own. We address misunderstandings and conflicts early, with clarity and forbearance. We help our partners become stronger companies, including by recommending them to other potential partners.

2. We avoid contracts or relationships that are based purely on transactional value to our firm, instead looking for vendors, partners, and investors whose practices we can reasonably assess for ethical intent. We sometimes forego the best available price in the short term in favor of a more redemptive venture's sustainability and mutual growth in the long term.

3. We are inclusive in our due diligence processes for partnerships (including investment), seeing these as crucial avenues of equity for under-represented groups. We push past the tendency to seek partnerships among those in our natural circles, instead taking initiative

to solicit who should have access to partnership but normally wouldn't.

4. We work diligently to be funded as much as possible by investors aligned on all three dimensions of our business: Strategy (desired impact through our venture, product, and mission); Operations (our intentions for team culture, partnerships, growth plans, and use of capital); and Leadership (personal goals, practices, and where appropriate, spiritual formation).

5. We take the risk of uncommon transparency and honesty with investors and other partners. We don't only provide investors with the good news; instead, in bold good faith, we appropriately share our successes, challenges, shifts in direction, and questions.

6. We build unusually generous equity structures. We see ownership as the highest level of partnership, and we look for creative and unexpected ways to involve more people in it, aiming to share in wealth creation with team members, key partners, those who generously helped us, and others who might not normally be on the cap table.

THE GOOD NEWS

Like great companies, great partnerships are fueled by an abundance mindset. The opportunities to create an ecosystem of abundance are in some ways even greater with our partners than with our team. Many are squeezed every day by owners, competitors, and customers who operate only from a mindset of scarcity and extraction. In our dealings with them we can be agents of hope, renewal, and sustainable energy for their own work and calling.

As we collaborate, we can be set free from the temptation and burden of territorialism—the need to count indicators of success in our field as belonging to us rather than to our mission. Indeed, we are set free from the tyranny of the word *our*, as if either the problem or the solution belonged to us. We will learn to prefer the wins we can share over the ones we can engineer alone.

This mindset, and the practices that flow from it, can lead to dramatic renewal in the sectors where we operate. A generous, patient, and trusting ecosystem of value creators will gradually grow, shifting the incentives for others in our economic "neighborhood." In the long run, we may not even get the credit for pioneering a new mutuality in our business sector—in fact, many of its benefits will come in the unseen form of exploitation, stress, and personal and business failures that simply never happened. But we will have been present at the beginning of a new way of stewarding value in our field.

We can also reasonably hope for investor relationships marked by trust and even friendship that is independent of the outcome of their investment. Because our journey of leadership is about who we are becoming as much as about what we are building—and because the same is true of their journey as investors—we can serve and relate to them on the basis of their unconditional worth, rather than on the terms of their financial worth.

AMBITION

WE SURRENDER OUR PERSONAL AMBITION TO GOD AND SEEK FIRST THE GOOD OF OTHERS

SUMMARY

We surrender our personal ambition to God and seek first the good of others, not ourselves. Instead of privately yielding our desires to an accumulation of wealth, power, and prestige, we cultivate gratitude, joy, and humility in the way we lead and serve.

OUR REALITY

As entrepreneurial leaders we long to build a business that can meet needs, address problems, provide meaningful work, and generate returns. We relish the satisfactions of entrepreneurship: inexhaustible energy for the mission; rapid learning curves; authorship of an organizational narrative; innovation in problem solving and venture building; delight in customer traction; and solidarity with others in the effort. We sense God's power at work through our leadership.

Yet we must acknowledge that we are seduced by a "winner's script" of how to scale a vision into the world through business. This script exalts certain goals (power, wealth, prestige, legacy) and prescribes the path to achieve them (audacious hustle, maniacal focus, maximum velocity, ruthless competition, elite backers). It has so much cultural power that it is hard for us to hold any counterscript in our imagination long enough to chart a different course.

Even Ethical versions of this script promise that we can "do well by doing good." We deeply hope this can be true of us; yet we also feel the force of Matthew 6, where we are warned of our inability to serve both God and money, and Mark 10, where we sense the weight of the rich young ruler's dilemma. Indeed, one of the greatest challenges we face as business builders is how to wrestle down the power of Mammon in our own imagination.

We are also seduced by the belief that the founder and venture are one. Our financial and growth metrics can feel like a referendum on our worth as a leader. The stewardship mentality we aspire to gradually tightens into an ownership mentality, and our belief in the mission becomes inextricable from our belief in ourselves.

This conflict arises from a distortion of our identity relative to our venture and its mission. We "know" that our true identity rests in Christ and not in our association with this organization. We "know" that whatever our ownership stake in the business may be, we are stewards and not owners of the mission, brand, and team. We "know" that our ambition must be surrendered to God's purposes. Yet our hearts are so susceptible to the pull of these false narratives—the myth of progress, the supremacy of money, and the conflation of our venture's success with our personal worth.

Instead, we long for God's love to perpetually re-orient us to his upside-down kingdom—first in our hearts, then through our leadership.

REDEMPTIVE OPPORTUNITIES

1. We use our power for the sake of others, not for our own benefit. We use our networks, influence, and time to generate opportunities for others, particularly those with limited access and agency. As we take calculated risks to deliver impact and returns, we absorb the downside vulnerability of these risks, and generously share the upside and credit with our team.

2. We actively create ways for others to glean opportunities for growth and satisfaction that might

otherwise be ours—for example, delegating not merely the tasks and roles we don't enjoy, but also some that we prefer to do ourselves. Over time we narrow our scope and focus of contribution so that "we are only doing what only we can do."

3. Understanding that our ambition creates pressure for many people besides ourselves, in both healthy and unhealthy ways, we give others a voice in our vision. Before committing to ambitious goals, we involve the people who must work to meet those goals. We bring our most consequential decisions before God and others—not making decisions by committee, but informing them through community.

4. We set patterns early on that acknowledge our limits and demonstrate that the mission can advance without us. We moderate our participation in the privileges of personal visibility, such as public speaking or writing engagements. Recognizing that we will be treated as experts, we position ourselves as learners inside and beyond the organization.

5. We prepare ourselves to share our faith as we "give the reason for the hope that we have" (1 Peter 3:15) in ways that provide clarity and invite accountability, without judgment or coercion of others. We connect our faith to our redemptive vision and commitments for the venture as suggested in this playbook, as well as our personal and leadership behavior and decisions.

6. Recognizing that our identity, motives, and imagination are the lifeblood and limiters of our organization's redemptive possibility, we attend urgently to our spiritual and moral formation. We make ourselves accountable to our team, board, and (where appropriate) our investors, submitting ourselves transparently to wise counsel, grace, and truth. We consider personally practicing Praxis's *A Rule of Life for Redemptive Entrepreneurs* to protect our entrepreneurial capacities.

THE GOOD NEWS

Before the redemptive pattern of creative restoration through sacrifice can take shape in the organization, it must take root in the leader's life. With us, this is impossible, but with God, all things are possible.

Leaders of redemptive ventures can experience greater abundance and peace as we trust in God—not ourselves, not in markets, not in technological advances or social progress—as the supreme actor in our business. We will lead with a high tolerance for healthy risk, knowing that our ultimate identity and provision does not ultimately depend on our "success" in the world's eyes. We will be able to hustle and compete joyfully, without malice or fear. With a settled posture of stewardship rather than ownership of our venture's resources, we can enjoy healthy and interdependent relationships with our investors, and remain more motivated by the mission than the exit.

The best news is that while this vocation is important, its stakes are not ultimate in our lives. We are not made righteous by our company's virtuous product design, our spotlessly ethical supply chain, our generous cap table, or even our sacrificial leadership—any more than we would be made righteous by an eight-figure exit or an invitation to Davos. As eager as we may be to bring good to the world, we will invariably fall short of expectations, and unwittingly disappoint and even harm others. We will encounter pain, setbacks, despair, and failure. Indeed, all these may come to pass, as they did for many of the prophets, the biblical character Job, and Jesus himself—even when we have been as faithful as we could possibly have been. We can face these experiences not as amputations of our identity, but as opportunities to be formed into our true identity in Christ.

Indeed, with love at the core of our business's mission, we will be able to experience any decision, any conversation, any win or loss as a sacred opportunity. Whether our business grows or dies; whether we exit with millions or debt; whether we change our corner of the world profoundly or not at all—we can know that God is with us and for us, offering us the profound invitation to be co-creators with him in the world.

A RULE OF LIFE FOR REDEMPTIVE ENTREPRENEURS

TIME

Instead of endless productivity, we practice a rhythm of work and rest, attending to our need to grow in all the dimensions of being human: heart, soul, mind, and strength. We commit to take one full day every week for complete rest from our daily work, and to make Sabbath possible for everyone within our sphere of authority.

MONEY

Instead of being preoccupied with money and possessions, we practice simplicity and generosity. We commit to give away a minimum of 10% of our gross income, with special attention to the needs of the materially poor.

IMAGINATION

Instead of having our imagination saturated by media, we seek to be transformed by the renewing of our mind. We commit to establish structured limits for our use of screens and our consumption of entertainment, in quantity, frequency, and moral character.

For the full Rule of Life for Redemptive Entrepreneurs:
rule.praxislabs.org

DECISION-MAKING

Instead of willful autonomy in decision making, we practice active dependence on God. We commit to daily prayer, and at times of major decisions, making every effort not to proceed until we have actively submitted our own desires about the decision fully to the will of God.

POWER

Instead of accumulating power to benefit ourselves or exploit others, we use it to generate possibility for those who have less access to opportunity. We commit to the practice of gleaning — frequently sacrificing opportunities for our own advancement to intentionally create pathways for others. We also practice chastity and fidelity, honoring the men and women with whom we work.

COMMUNITY

Instead of individualism and isolation, we practice real presence with others who are not part of our daily work. We pursue diversity across class and ethnicity in our friendships and mentoring relationships.

Our goal with this playbook has been to capture the redemptive spirit and practices of the real-life founders and mentors in the Praxis community and beyond. Thanks to all of them for their faithful and visionary work.

Special thanks to the leaders who provided active contributions: Ben Chelf, Haley Robison Dake, Ben Fischer, Donna Harris, Will Haughey, Jessica Kim, Debbie McCoy, Justin Straight, and Bernard Worthy.

This book was authored by Praxis Partners Dave Blanchard, Andy Crouch, and Scott Kauffmann.

Praxis is a creative engine for redemptive entrepreneurship, supporting founders, funders, and innovators motivated by their faith to love their neighbors and renew culture.

redemptivebusiness.com
praxislabs.org

Made in United States
Orlando, FL
18 December 2022